WHAT THE FUTURE HOLDS

THE FUTURE OF ENERGY:

FROM SOLAR CELLS TO FLYING WIND FARMS

BY M. M. EBOCH
CONTENT CONSULTANT:
PETER C. BISHOP, PH.D., APF
TEACH THE FUTURE.ORG
HOUSTONFUTURES.ORG

CAPSTONE PRESS
a capstone imprint

Capstone Captivate is published by Capstone Press, an imprint of Capstone.
1710 Roe Crest Drive, North Mankato, Minnesota 56003
www.capstonepub.com

Copyright © 2020 by Capstone. All rights reserved. No part of this publication may be reproduced in whole or in part, or stored in a retrieval system, or transmitted in any form or by any means, electronic, mechanical, photocopying, recording, or otherwise, without written permission of the publisher.

Library of Congress Cataloging-in-Publication Data is available on the Library of Congress website.
ISBN: 978-1-5435-9220-7 (library binding)
ISBN: 978-1-4966-6624-6 (paperback)
ISBN: 978-1-5435-9224-5 (eBook PDF)

Summary: Describes what the future may hold in the realm of energy, including technological advancements and human impact.

Image Credits
Alamy: dpa picture alliance, 27; AP Images: Marty Lederhandler, 35 (bottom), Robert F. Bukaty, 21; NASA, 17, 35 (top); Newscom: imageBROKER/Michael Peuckert, 43, ZUMA Press/Connie Zhou, 31; Science Source: CLAUS LUNAU, 39, Peggy Greb/USDA, 25; Shutterstock: Evgeny Vorobyev, 15, Gary Whitton, 7, JoshuaDaniel, 11, Monkey Business Images, 5, NadyGinzburg, 9, Peteri, 29, PopTika, Cover, Ryan Janssens, 23, T.W. van Urk, 13, Wead, 37, yotily, 19, Zbynek Burival, 41; Wikimedia: Olivierabristol, 33

Design Elements
Shutterstock: nanmulti, Zeynur Babayev

Editorial Credits
Editor: Mandy Robbins; Designer: Kay Fraser; Media Researcher: Jo Miller; Production Specialist: Laura Manthe

All internet sites appearing in back matter were available and accurate when this book was sent to press.

Printed in the United States   5443

TABLE OF CONTENTS

INTRODUCTION
A GROWING NEED FOR POWER 4

CHAPTER 1
WHAT IS JUST AHEAD? 8

CHAPTER 2
WHAT DOES THE FUTURE HOLD?........................ 20

CHAPTER 3
WHAT IS WAY OUT THERE? 32

TIMELINE 44
GLOSSARY 46
READ MORE 47
INTERNET SITES 47
INDEX........................ 48

Words in bold are in the glossary.

INTRODUCTION
A GROWING NEED FOR POWER

Think of all the things you use that need **electricity**. Electricity turns on the lights. It can be used to heat and cool buildings. It charges cell phones. It runs computers, microwaves, refrigerators, and more.

Yet the use of electricity is fairly new. The first U.S. **power plants** opened in 1882. They each served only a few buildings. In 1925, half of the homes in the United States had electricity. Now few homes are without it.

Electricity changed society in huge ways. It is easier and safer than using candles, oil lamps, or open fires. Many modern devices won't work without it. Our power use grows every year as we get more devices and use them more often. At the same time, the world's population is growing. More people using more technology means a greater need for power. People in the U.S. now use 16 times more electricity than they did in 1950. How can we keep up with this demand?

Look around your kitchen. How many electrical devices do you see?

FACT

Energy cannot be created or destroyed. It can be transferred, and it can change forms. It can also be stored over time.

HOW WE MAKE ELECTRICITY

The sun is a huge source of energy. Plants and animals take in energy from the sun. They store that energy in chemical form. When they die, the energy gets changed to other forms. Some plants and animals that died long ago broke down to become coal, oil, and natural gas. These substances are called **fossil fuels**. They are formed from the remains of living things from long ago. Most of our energy today comes from fossil fuels. That's likely to be true for many years. But we can't count on fossil fuels forever.

Many power plants burn fossil fuels. Doing this converts stored chemical energy to heat energy. The heat is used to boil water and make steam. That's how the heat energy changes into kinetic energy, or the energy of motion. In the form of steam, tiny water droplets race through the air. The moving steam turns a large fan, called a **turbine**. A **generator** then converts the motion energy into electrical energy. Electrical energy can move through wires to wherever we need it.

Power plants create energy people can use, but burning fossil fuels releases smoke that is harmful to the environment.

FACT
Like electricity, natural gas can be sent directly into buildings. Then it may be used for heat or to power appliances such as gas stoves.

CHAPTER 1
WHAT IS JUST AHEAD?

Earth has limited amounts of fossil fuels. People could run out of them in the next 100 years. Plus, burning fossil fuels causes **pollution**. Using fossil fuels is harmful to human health and to the environment. It adds to **climate change**.

Knowing what may happen in the future helps us decide what to do now. Scientists study how the environment is changing. They predict what will happen if we keep using fossil fuels. Then they can suggest changes for a healthier future.

We must switch to different ways of making electricity. We have many alternatives to fossil fuels. Some power plants don't need to burn coal or natural gas. These power plants cause less pollution. They use **renewable energy**, so they will never run out. These forms of energy are growing in popularity.

Most vehicles use gasoline, a product made from oil. Oil is a fossil fuel.

FACT
Nearly half of Americans live in areas with unhealthy air. Cars and other vehicles are the worst polluters.

ENERGY INSIDE THE EARTH

The inside of Earth is very hot. In some places, underground water is nearly 1,800 degrees Fahrenheit (1,000 degrees Celsius). **Geothermal** power uses this heat from inside our planet. If the water is close enough to the surface, a well can tap it. The hot water comes up and turns to steam. That steam turns turbines. Making electricity this way skips the step of burning fossil fuels.

Geothermal plants release harmless steam. Most of the water can be pumped back into the ground. There it can pick up more heat and be used again.

Geothermal power is mainly used where hot water comes near the surface. In the near future, deeper wells could reach Earth's heat in more areas. The deepest wells planned now are 2.8 miles (4.5 kilometers) deep. Companies hope to dig even deeper wells soon. Deeper wells mean more heat and more power.

The Ohaaki Power Station in New Zealand taps into local geothermal resources.

FACT
Earth's heat sometimes reaches the surface in hot springs or volcanoes. These features show where geothermal resources can be found.

ENERGY FROM THE AIR

Wind energy is another popular option for the future. Wind turbines don't need steam to move them. They use the power of the blowing wind. This saves a step and does not release pollutants from burning fossil fuels. Wind is free and will never run out.

Wind power works best where the wind is strong and steady. The wind is stronger and steadier high above the ground. Taller towers with longer blades can capture this wind. One planned wind turbine will reach more than 850 feet (260 meters) tall. However, tall, skinny things tend to bend in high winds. Blades can twist and destroy the turbine. Engineers must find ways to make the turbines strong enough to withstand strong winds.

Ocean wind is also stronger and steadier than wind on land. It is more expensive to build wind farms in the ocean, but they can produce more power. Many countries are building wind farms near the coast. In the U.S., at least 15 projects are planned. Designers in Massachusetts hope to have 84 offshore wind turbines up and running by 2022.

The Netherlands has wind turbines both on land and offshore.

WORKING WITH WATER

A rushing river also has a lot of motion energy. At a **hydropower** plant, a dam built across a river directs the water into a tunnel. The water turns a turbine to make electricity, and then it flows downstream.

Hydropower supplies electricity to more than 1 billion people around the world. In Canada, nearly 60 percent of electricity comes from water. Norway, Brazil, and the Democratic Republic of the Congo use even more. Ninety percent of their electricity comes from water.

The U.S. has 80,000 dams. Most were built to control flooding or bring water to people and farm fields. Only 3 percent are now used for power. Building new dams is expensive, but hydropower could be added to more of the dams that exist now. Plans are underway to convert 32 U.S. dams to hydropower. Thousands more could be converted in the future. Hydropower makes only about 7 percent of U.S. electricity. That number should grow as hydropower is added to more dams.

The Krasnoyarsk Dam creates electricity from the power of the Yenisei River in Siberia, Russia.

USING THE SUN'S RAYS

Some renewable energies don't use turbines at all. Solar energy uses panels to capture sunlight, a form of heat energy. The panels convert the sun's heat energy to electric energy. Groups of large solar panels can provide power to a town. Small panels can power small devices such as calculators. Solar panels can power the lights on city streets. They can charge electric vehicles in public parking lots. The International Space Station (ISS) even uses solar power.

New companies are experimenting with solar windows and even solar paint. Solar windows capture some of the sun's energy for power but also allow light to pass through. Solar paint could turn almost any surface into a power source. With solar windows and paint, buildings could make power to run lights and machines inside.

FACT
Electric vehicles are usually plugged in to charge. New solar panels can go on cars so they get power from the sun too.

POWERING REMOTE LOCATIONS

In some countries, power plants only provide electricity to big cities. People who live far from cities need another way to get power. Millions of homes in Asia and Africa now use solar panels. Solar panels power schools and health clinics in remote areas.

The solar panels on the ISS can collect solar energy for longer periods of time per day than solar panels on Earth can.

ENERGY FROM ATOMS

Nuclear power splits **atoms** to create nuclear reactions. These reactions release energy and make heat. Many countries use nuclear power. In the United States, almost 20 percent of electricity comes from it.

Nuclear power does not pollute the air. However, it does produce deadly waste, which must be stored safely. Many people are afraid of nuclear power. No one wants nuclear waste near where they live, so the waste is piling up. Even worse, a damaged nuclear power plant can release poisons. Large disasters have killed people and polluted big areas.

Nuclear power at its best is clean, efficient, and cheap to produce once the expense of building the plant is covered. Some experts say nuclear power is the best bet for the future.

The latest nuclear plants recycle used fuel. By doing this, they make more energy and leave less dangerous waste. Russia started using the first of these power plants in 2015. Taking steps to solve the waste problem gives nuclear energy a safer future.

The Tihange Nuclear Power Station in Belgium has three nuclear power plants.

FACT

In 2011, an earthquake caused a series of large waves called a tsunami to hit Japan. A nuclear power plant that was destroyed released deadly pollution.

CHAPTER 2
WHAT DOES THE FUTURE HOLD?

What happens if we look further into the future? Some forms of renewable energy have potential, but they're not working well yet. The next 30 years may prove whether these ideas take off or fade.

The first offshore wind farm in the U.S. started working in 2016. A dozen more were soon planned. Most projects are on the East Coast.

People in California are interested in offshore wind too. However, the water off the West Coast is deeper. Turbines attached to the ocean floor wouldn't reach above the water to the wind. Floating wind turbines may solve this problem. Currently, 14 companies are designing floating turbines. They would work on the West Coast where the ocean is deep. However, the designs have yet to prove they will work. The earliest tests might start in 2025.

DO LESS HARM

Even renewable energy has downsides, particularly to animals. Wind turbines on land can kill bats and birds. Turbines in the ocean might harm marine animals. We can lessen the damage with careful design and planning. For example, fewer birds die if wind turbines are not built in common travel paths of birds.

The first offshore wind turbine in the United States was installed off the coast of Castine, Maine, in 2013.

RUSHING IN AND OUT

Ocean winds have power, and so do ocean waves. Tidal power uses energy from ocean water. Tidal power can be captured with turbines similar to wind turbines. These turbines are attached to the ocean floor near the coastline, where tides rush in and out. The force of the ocean current turns the blades.

Tidal turbines must withstand ocean storms. They must not be damaged by salty seawater. These are tough challenges. Scotland and South Korea are successfully using tidal turbines. Wave power could produce twice the electricity the world now makes. But it doesn't work well everywhere yet.

In the U.S., the Ocean Power Energy Company built the first commercial tidal power project in Maine. However, the tides were not strong enough to produce the desired power. The company decided to end the project and remove the turbines. Other states on both the West and East Coasts have considered projects for tidal power. None are in progress yet.

People see the power of tidal waves from above. But tidal power turbines would be beneath the water's surface.

FACT
Waves also have energy in the up-and-down motion of the water. Devices that float on top of the water can capture that wave energy.

PLANTS AS FUEL

Biofuel uses matter from living things, such as plants, as fuel. This fuel is often used to power vehicles. It is burned to make steam that turns turbines. It sounds just like using fossil fuels. But this system burns new plants instead of ancient plants. Plants are renewable, so we can quickly grow more of them. Biofuel does release pollution when it is burned. But plants absorb CO2, the main gas that causes climate change. The growing plants help clean the air.

In the United States, most biofuel is made from corn. In Brazil, many cars run on fuel made from sugarcane. Europe uses a fuel often made from palm oil. But some experts say we should not use food crops for fuel. It uses too much land and water. Turning the plants into fuels takes a lot of energy as well.

That doesn't mean biofuel won't work. College students in Massachusetts found a way to get more energy out of biofuel from food scraps. Restaurants and grocery stores end up with many food scraps and used cooking oil. They could be turned into biofuel.

Engineers Neil Goldberg (left) and Akwasi Boateng (right) built a machine that converts crop leftovers into renewable energy.

POOP FUEL

What else could we use as fuel? How about toilet waste? Wastewater, or sewage, is water left over from other uses, such as baths, laundry, and washing dishes. It also includes what is flushed down the toilet. Wastewater must be cleaned, or it can pollute local water supplies.

Alabama built the world's first algae biofuel system. In this system, plastic bags are filled with wastewater. Algae, which are tiny plants, are added to the bags. The algae feed off the wastewater, which cleans the water. Then the algae are used as biofuel. The cleaned water flows into the local bay. This solves two problems. It cleans dirty water, and it makes cheap fuel.

Some experts thought we would be making billions of gallons of fuel from algae before now. Instead, many algae biofuel companies have failed. While this type of fuel holds so much promise, it is simply too expensive to produce at this point. A few companies are still trying. Synthetic Genomics has partnered with oil company ExxonMobil. They hope to produce 10,000 barrels of algae biofuel a day by 2025.

Researchers at the Institute for Bio and Geosciences in Germany are working on making biofuel from algae more efficient.

FACT

Astronauts need to recycle wastewater in space. The United States space agency, NASA is working on a system to clean wastewater with algae.

IS SMALLER BETTER?

People often look for big solutions to big problems. But sometimes the solution is to go smaller. Today most power plants are huge and wasteful. They must send their energy long distances. Doing that is difficult and expensive. In the future, each city and town could have its own small power plant. That way, energy wouldn't be wasted traveling long distances.

With small local power plants, communities could use whatever energy source works best at that location. Even individual homes and businesses could generate part of their own power. Coastal cities and towns could run on tidal power. Towns with geothermal resources could tap that for power. Inland towns in flat areas could run on wind power. Desert locations could use solar power.

The town of Pilsen in the Czech Republic has a solar power station.

USE LESS, SAVE MORE

We can save energy in small ways too. Turn off lights in an empty room. Turn off devices you're not using. Each of us can help in little ways.

Artificial intelligence (AI) can turn small savings into big results. Artificial intelligence uses computers to make decisions. In a building, AI can monitor lights, heat, and appliances. It makes changes to keep people comfortable while using less energy.

Google has many large groups of computers. They need to stay cool or the computers will fail. The company trusted AI to judge how much cooling was needed. Google cut the amount of energy used to cool its computers by 40 percent.

A company called DeepMind made the system Google used. The United Kingdom's power company National Grid is considering using DeepMind to help cut its energy use as well. The whole country might start using AI to control its power. Other countries and companies could follow.

Google data centers, such as this one in Council Bluffs, Iowa, are located around the world.

CHAPTER 3
WHAT IS WAY OUT THERE?

The further ahead we look, the more difficult predictions become. What could the world look like in 50 or 100 years? Scientists and engineers constantly explore new paths. Some ideas seem unlikely. Yet these creative ideas could solve the world's energy problems.

FLYING WIND FARMS

Air currents are stronger and steadier high above ground. But tower turbines have height limits. The company Altaeros Energies has a solution. It is building wind turbines that fly! These turbines could make two or three times the energy of ground wind turbines.

Go high enough, and winds can reach more than 100 miles (160 km) per hour. But that requires reaching a height of 20,000 to 50,000 feet (6,000 to 15,000 m). Reaching those winds brings many challenges. For one, airplanes fly in that range. Flying wind farms would have to stay out of flight paths.

FACT
The winds high above the ground could provide 100 times the energy the world needs.

The Kiwee One is a flying, wind-powered generator developed by French company Kitewinder.

SOLAR ENERGY IN SPACE

Solar energy is also more powerful high above ground. In space, it's never cloudy or rainy. Much more solar energy could be captured there. But how do we get the energy to the ground?

Scientists have built one model showing how this could work in the future. A tile would capture sunlight and convert it to electricity. The electricity would then be converted to radio waves. An antenna would send the energy to Earth. A receiver on the ground would capture the waves. They would then be turned back into electricity. Other ideas suggest using microwaves or lasers instead of radio waves.

So far the model has only been tested in a lab. Many questions remain. Will the system be safe? Can the tiles be made light enough? Would it be affordable to get them into space? Currently, it costs thousands of dollars to send 2 pounds (1 kilogram) of material into space. A space-based energy system could cost more than $36 billion to build.

Solar panels only work when the sun is shining. Putting them in space would generate more electricity than they do on Earth.

FACT
Author Isaac Asimov came up with the idea of space-based solar power in 1941. He used it in his science-fiction short story, "Reason."

SUPER VOLCANIC HEAT

Geothermal power already uses heat from underground. Sometimes this heat reaches Earth's surface in a volcano. In the distant future, scientists could figure out how to harness volcanic energy for human use.

A supervolcano is a very large volcano capable of huge eruptions. Our planet has 20 known supervolcanoes. No supervolcano is likely to erupt in the next 100 years. But if one did, it could change the climate. Food crops could fail. People could starve.

One supervolcano is under Yellowstone National Park. NASA wants to stop this volcano from erupting. NASA has proposed turning Yellowstone into a geothermal power plant. Pumping water into the **magma** chamber would cool the volcano. The water could pick up heat and return to the surface. We could use that heat for energy. Once the volcano is cooled enough, it should not erupt.

Italy's Mount Etna erupted in 2014, releasing a huge amount of heat energy. In the future, humans could convert this type of energy to electricity.

CHALLENGES OF VOLCANIC POWER

Using Yellowstone as a volcanic power plant has many risks, though. The most dangerous is that trying to stop the volcano might actually set it off. Drilling into the magma chamber could release harmful gases. It could make the cap over the magma chamber more brittle. Then that cap could crack, releasing lava. Experts at NASA think they can avoid this. They would drill from the lower sides to get under the magma chamber.

But there are more challenges. The magma chamber under Yellowstone is very deep. Workers would need to pump water down 6 miles (10 km). That's much farther than anyone has drilled before.

Cost would pose a challenge too. The project is estimated to cost almost $3.5 billion. Selling the energy would pay for that over time. But this initial money would have to come from somewhere.

The magma chamber beneath Yellowstone National Park has several different sections.

TINY POWERS

Not every new idea means going into space or deep underground. Small power devices could change the future too.

People are constantly moving. Something called a piezoelectric device makes small amounts of electricity when it is bent or pressed. It can be powered by a person walking. College research labs have made these devices. They are not available for sale yet. Someday we may use such devices to charge our cell phones and smart watches as we move.

Another device makes power through static electricity. Snow carries a positive electrical charge. The snow TENG device is made out of a material with a negative charge. It captures the positive charge from snow. It combines those charges into electricity. Scientists at UCLA made the first snow TENG with a 3-D printer. No company is making the devices to sell yet. But someday snow-powered devices could be added to solar panels. The result would work in sun or snow.

When solar panels are covered in snow, they don't work.
The snow TENG device could solve that problem.

LOOKING AHEAD

Can we stop using fossil fuels? Some places already have. Iceland gets all its energy from other sources. It uses hydropower and geothermal power. Costa Rica and Norway use almost all renewable energy too.

In the United States, Georgetown, Texas, currently gets all its energy from wind turbines and solar panels. The town of 67,000 people is the largest U.S. city using only renewable energy, though the costs have proven challenging. Many other U.S. cities hope to switch entirely to renewable energy. Plans often call for making the switch within 10 to 20 years.

For more than 100 years, many people have said we need to change our energy sources. Inventor Alexander Graham Bell addressed this in a 1917 speech. He thought it might be possible to get energy from the tides, waves, or the sun's rays. Today we can do all that. Only time will tell what the future holds. Scientists continue to make great strides in the area of renewable energy.

FACT

Hawaii hopes to use only local renewable energy by 2045. The state's many volcanoes make geothermal power a good option.

Ljósafoss Power Station is one of Iceland's many renewable energy power plants.

TIMELINE

6000 BC People use sails to harness wind energy for transportation.

500 BC The Chinese use natural gas leaking from the ground to boil water.

AD 1100 Windmills in Europe harness wind power to grind grain.

1690 Coal begins to replace wood as fuel in Europe, due to forests being cut down.

1850–1945 The primary fuel source in the U.S. is coal. Natural gas is also used for lighting and wood for heating.

1859 The first oil well in the United States is drilled in Pennsylvania.

1868 The first modern solar power plant is used to heat water for a steam engine in Algeria, Africa.

1882 The world's first commercial hydropower plant starts in Wisconsin.

1888 The first windmill used to generate electricity is developed in Ohio.

1925 Half of homes in the United States have electric power.

1935 Hoover Dam, the world's largest hydropower plant, is built.

1938 German scientist Otto Hahn discovers the process for nuclear energy.

1950 Oil-based fuels become the most used fuels in the United States.

1951 The first nuclear power plant is built in Idaho.

1974 The solar-cell device is developed in the U.S.

1980 The world's first wind farm is built in New Hampshire.

1981 The first large-scale solar power plant starts working in California.

2014 Alabama builds the world's first algae biofuel system.

2016 The first offshore wind farm in the U.S. starts working.

GLOSSARY

artificial intelligence (ar-ti-FISH-uhl in-TEL-uh-junss)—the ability of a machine to imitate human behavior

atom (AT-uhm)—an element in its smallest form

biofuel (BYE-oh-fyoo-uhl)—a fuel made of, or produced from, plant material

climate change (KLY-muht CHAYNJ)—a significant change in Earth's climate over a period of time

electricity (i-lek-TRISS-uh-tee)—a natural force used to make light and heat or to make machines work

fossil fuel (FAH-suhl FYOOL)—natural fuel formed from the remains of plants and animals

generator (JEN-uh-ray-tur)—a machine used to convert mechanical energy into electricity

geothermal (jee-oh-THUR-muhl)—heat inside the earth

hydropower (HY-druh-pow-uhr)—the production of electricity from moving water

magma (MAG-muh)—melted rock beneath Earth's crust

nuclear (NOO-klee-ur)—describes energy converted by splitting two particles of matter

pollution (puh-LOO-shuhn)—harmful materials that damage the air, water, and soil

power plant (POW-ur PLANT)—a building or group of buildings used to create electricity

renewable energy (ri-NOO-uh-buhl EN-er-jee)—power from sources that will not be used up

turbine (TUR-bine)—a machine with blades that can be turned by a moving fluid such as steam or water

READ MORE

Green, Dan. *Energy.* New York: DK Children, 2016.

Hawbaker, Emily. *Energy Lab for Kids: 40 Exciting Experiments to Explore, Create, Harness, and Unleash Energy.* Beverly, MA: Quarry Books, 2017.

Sneideman, Joshua. *Renewable Energy: Discover the Fuel of the Future With 20 Projects.* Norwich, VT: Nomad Press, 2016.

INTERNET SITES

Alliant Energy Kids
www.alliantenergykids.com/

Science Kids: Energy Facts
www.sciencekids.co.nz/sciencefacts/energy.html

The U.S. Energy Information Administration: Energy Explained
www.eia.gov/energyexplained/

INDEX

algae, 26, 27
artificial intelligence (AI), 30

biofuel, 24, 26

climate change, 8, 24

flying wind farms, 32
fossil fuels, 6, 8, 10, 12, 24, 42
   coal, 6, 8
   natural gas, 6, 7, 8
   oil, 6, 24, 26

geothermal energy, 10, 11, 28, 36, 42, 43

hydropower, 14, 42

International Space Station (ISS), 16

nuclear power, 18, 19

offshore wind farms, 12, 20

piezoelectric device, 40
pollution, 8, 9, 12, 18, 19, 24, 26

snow TENG device, 40
solar power, 16, 17, 28, 34, 40, 42
   space-based, 34, 35

tidal power, 22, 23, 28, 42

volcanoes, 11, 36, 38, 43

wind power, 12, 20, 21, 22, 28, 42

Yellowstone National Park, 36, 38